The Well-Stocked Granary

The Well-Stocked Granary

A guide to personal pension plans and savings schemes for the self-employed

Tessa Morrison

Illustrated by Arthur Robins

Hutchinson Benham, London

For the self-employed, planning for retirement is an off-putting business. All those bewildering pension and savings schemes conspire to put you off, so you put them off.

Books on investment may only hasten this process. Pages of figures, charts and diagrams, far from aiding comprehension, merely complicate matters further.

This book attempts to put serious practical information in a different context.

This book was sponsored by the
Provident Mutual Life Assurance Association,
25-31 Moorgate, London EC2,
and conceived by PVAF Advertising

The few figures quoted in this book were correct at the time of going to press, although some are likely to change as time passes. Taken as a whole they should prove useful from a comparative standpoint, even when certain figures are no longer up to date

Hutchinson Benham Ltd
3 Fitzroy Square, London W1P 6JD

London Melbourne Sydney Auckland Wellington Johannesburg
and agencies throughout the world

First published 1979

Set in Century Schoolbook by Owl Creative Services Limited

Printed in Great Britain by the Anchor Press Ltd
and bound by Wm Brendon & Son Ltd, both of Tiptree, Essex

ISBN 0 09 138980 1 cased
0 09 138981 X paper

Contents

Introduction: 'Go to the ant, thou sluggard; consider her ways and be wise'

Solomon: PROVERBS vi. 6

The self-employed viewed retirement with trepidation even in ancient times. What was there to look forward to at the end of a carefree career as an apothecary or a freelance harpist? Nothing but a penniless, cheerless old age.

A few optimists, convinced that somehow, somewhere there had to be an alternative to this grim fate, looked up Solomon for advice, only to discover that the solution to their problem lay in their local ant-hill. Still mystified after several painstaking days of ant observation, they heaved a collective sigh and resorted to Aesop. Although he was long-winded, his explanatory fables were at least crystal clear.

'One bright winter's day', he related, 'a group of industrious ants were drying out some of their carefully harvested grain which had got wet in a thunderstorm. Along came a desperately thin grasshopper, a mere shadow of his former exuberant self, begging them pitifully for a morsel to eat.

'They asked him what he was up to all summer. Surely he'd made some provision for the winter by stocking up his granary? The grasshopper shook his head wretchedly and confessed that he'd felt so light-hearted in the summer months that he had spent every available moment singing.

'At this the ants would have no further truck with him. "Well", they retorted, "if you were imprudent enough to spend the whole summer singing, we suggest you go off and spend the whole winter dancing". And they turned their backs on him as he sloped miserably away.

'This is the wisdom of the ant that Solomon would have you imitate: stock your granary well in the summer of your life and you will avoid the grasshopper's winter of distress. In other words, put aside part of your earnings during your working life and you'll have adequate funds to help you enjoy your declining years.'

To the self-employed of today, what was once a revelation is now no more than an obvious course to follow. The trouble is that post-biblical times have so complicated the process of granary-stocking that it's hard to know just how to set about it.

Retiring once used to mean just that: withdrawing from a useful active life through sheer incapacity. Even in Shakespeare's time a man who downed tools was well on the way to 'second childishness and mere oblivion; sans teeth, sans eyes, sans taste, sans–everything'. As such, his needs were not excessive.

But consider his modern counterpart—still sprightly, looking forward to a new lease of life, and more than likely to race past the old three-score-and-ten mark—and you'll see that nowadays it takes a considerable amount of financial grain-storing to fund one's retirement.

Alas, gone are the simple days of horsehair mattresses lumpy with savings, superseded both by foam rubber and inflation. Today a bewildering number and variety of pension plans and other investment schemes vie with one another to unit-link your input and escalate your outflow. How on earth do you choose between them?

To confuse matters further the State incorporates a retirement pension within the range of benefits provided by the National Insurance scheme. How does this affect your personal provision?

The ramifications of a basically simple concept are now so impenetrable as to turn any self-employed person into a fervent grasshopper for life. It's time a logical, historical delve into the complexities of contemporary granaries restored the confidence of the self-employed in the continuing sagacity of the post-biblical ant.

The People's Budget
Whisky

1 The Welsh Wizard's war

In 1909 a fiery Welshman called David Lloyd George presented his first budget as Chancellor of the Exchequer. It had a far from rapturous reception in Parliament. The House of Lords was horrified by it. Lord Rosebery called it 'the negation of Faith, of Family, of Property, of Monarchy, of Empire'. The Irish Party was outraged. Lloyd George found himself vehemently attacked by the middle classes and his budget was actually flung out by the Lords – an unprecedented event.

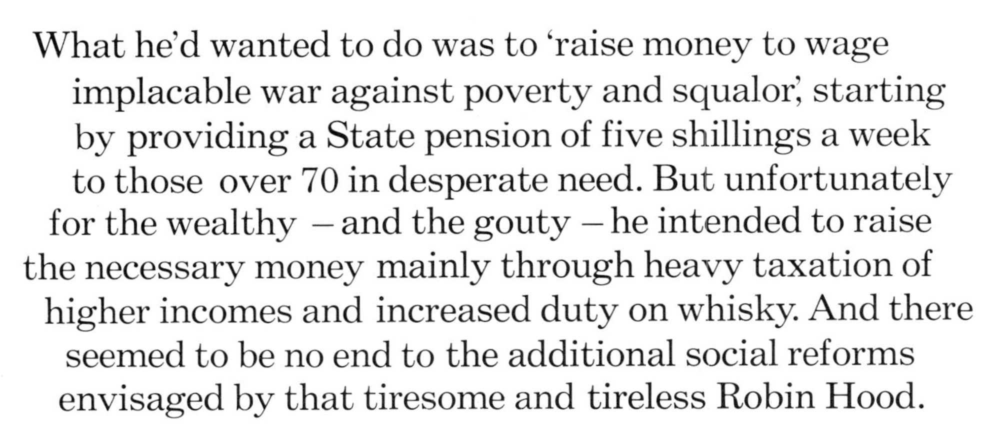

What he'd wanted to do was to 'raise money to wage implacable war against poverty and squalor', starting by providing a State pension of five shillings a week to those over 70 in desperate need. But unfortunately for the wealthy – and the gouty – he intended to raise the necessary money mainly through heavy taxation of higher incomes and increased duty on whisky. And there seemed to be no end to the additional social reforms envisaged by that tiresome and tireless Robin Hood.

Although five shillings amounted to no more than a sixth of the average weekly wage in 1909, it was to constitute a kind of salvation to an enormous number of impoverished people. This is evident from the heated

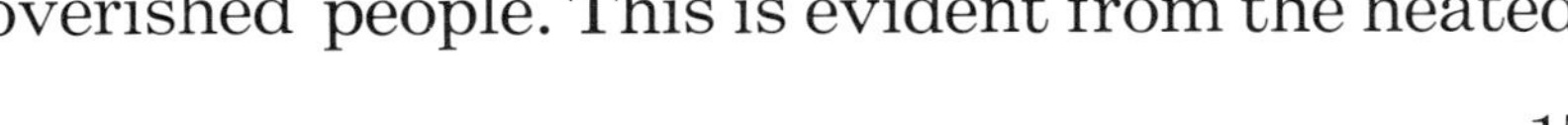

discussions on funding that took place over the next few days: it was estimated that six million pounds would need to be raised, but that much of this could come from the rates as many old people could now cease to be 'kept' by the workhouse . . . .

It was not for nothing that Lloyd George had christened his budget 'The People's Budget'; the majority of them showed their appreciation of his measures by voting his party back to power in the next General Election. Meanwhile, in wonderfully eloquent speeches, Lloyd George had been triumphantly ridiculing his attackers. Many of them got their most crushing come-uppance in 1911 when an Act was passed restricting the power of the Lords ('that sinister assembly') and making it impossible for them ever again to reject a money Bill.

The first battle in the Welsh Wizard's war was won. But the first pensions it produced, though a boon to the recipients, could do no more than scratch just part of the surface of the poverty problem. For a start the half a million pensions the State paid over the first year out of general taxation were a tremendous drain on resources, a liability that could only get worse. Then of course it wasn't only the over-70s who needed State aid—there were the sick and the unemployed, widows and orphans.

Lloyd George was the first to realize this. As early as 1911 he began to put matters right with his National Insurance Act. This didn't go down any better than his budget. Those self-same people who had cried blue murder at his plans to rob the rich now frenziedly denounced him for robbing the poor. His whole plan was considered simply preposterous.

His plan was a compulsory insurance scheme for the working classes. Initially they would be protected against sickness, disablement and unemployment (in certain cases), but later old age pensions and widows' and orphans' benefits could be provided in much the same way (this eventually happened in 1925).

All this was, of course, quite admirable. The snag was that the worker would be required to contribute fourpence a week into a benefit fund to help finance the operation. Those who beat their breasts at the mere concept of a worker forced to part with a weekly fourpence tended to overlook the origin of the rest of the fund: the man's employer was required to contribute 3d. and the State provided a further 2d. The cry went up of 'Ninepence for fourpence!'

Of course hindsight now shows us that 'Ninepence for fourpence!', far from constituting robbery of the poor, actually provided the only feasible long-term solution to the relief of distress on a national scale. The 'free' pension was a necessary stand-by for those already old and unable to provide for themselves, but the new contributory idea, already benefiting some 13½ million people by 1914, would eventually solve the problem of how to provide — among other benefits — pensions for future generations of the aged.

Lloyd George had always had this annoying tendency to be right, despite fierce opposition to his point of view. He had been the only one to stick his neck out and plead the Boers' case during the Boer War, only to be vindicated by history. History would appear to have upheld his stand in the war against poverty and squalor as well. Despite any amount of modifications and additions, the strategy he drew up a life-span ago is still recognizable in the National Insurance scheme of today.

PENSION

2 'I've got sixpence, jolly little si I've got sixpence to last me all my I've got tuppence to spend and tu and tuppence to take home to my

Millions of people today, including the self-employed, make a weekly contribution to the National Insurance fund. There's simply no way they can avoid it.

The fund they're helping to build up is currently providing all kinds of benefits for those covered by the scheme, from sickness, unemployment and maternity allowances to retirement pensions for the elderly.

Since retirement pensions are only a part of this comprehensive cover you might expect them to be less than lavish. You would not be wrong. The basic State retirement pension pays out a current weekly maximum of £19.50 to single people and £31.20 to married couples. Although as the years roll by these amounts will increase in line with prices or average earnings, whichever is the greater, their spending value will remain more or less unchanged. They are thus hardly likely to keep self-made men or women in the style to which they have become accustomed.

pence,
life,
pence to lend
wife’

In fact the self-employed do particularly badly out of the National Insurance scheme. For a start their weekly payment of £2.10,* although higher than that of any other class of contributor, does not entitle them to one of the major perks on offer – unemployment benefit.

Even worse, they do not qualify for any part of the additional State retirement pension, despite making an additional payment to the State of five per cent of their annual profits between £2250 and £7000.

This is not to say that the National Insurance scheme is a big waste of time and money for the self-employed. They are, after all, eligible for a whole series of useful, if unspectacular, grants and allowances,† for their families as well as for themselves: always provided that their contribution record is up to scratch.

The State is a real stickler for its own brand of fair-play. If you haven't clocked up the excessively complicated minimum number of contributions required for any benefit to be paid in full, you'll get only part of that benefit or nothing at all.

Unfortunately the contribution requirements for a full retirement pension are particularly stringent. You're expected to fork out a minimum annual sum, currently equal to more than six months of unfaltering weekly contributions, over 90 per cent of your so-called 'working life' – which actually

*Applies to annual earnings totalling over £1050. Voluntary contributions may be paid by those earning less than this amount to secure a retirement pension and other minor benefits.

†See under National Insurance Benefits in Glossary.

means from official school-leaving age (16) to official retirement age (65 for a man, 60 for a woman). Many an apparently regular contributor could therefore find to his surprise and consternation that his eagerly awaited pension arrives in a sadly depleted condition.

And that is assuming that there is still a government around when he retires, taking contributions from a new generation to provide him with his old age dues.

Avid readers of the occasional thrift columns of some evening papers and women's magazines, well versed in the arts of tea-bag recycling, hay-box cookery and spotting a bargain used garment at 500 paces, will no doubt find the financial constrictions of an uncertain State pension both a challenge and an incentive to further ingenious innovation.

Spiritual descendants of famous cheese-parers such as Colonel O'Dogherty or the King of Patterdale will also delight in its limitations. The former, though a wealthy landowner, lived in a windowless hut accessible only by a ladder and went about his frugal business dressed in rags, wearing an old night-cap for a wig, topped by a tattered brimless hat. The latter, resident in slightly grander squalor at the head of Lake Ullswater, had an income of £800 a year but never spent more than £30. His last words at the age of 89 were, 'What a fortune a man might make if he lived to the age of Methuselah!'

Those who fancy that fortune, but wish to acquire it in somewhat less straitened circumstances, may care to look further afield for a top-up of the State-run granary.

3 May the worst man win

Ever since the dawn of money the idea of receiving a tidy little fortune on a regular yearly basis for the rest of one's life has proved a tantalizing dream. And as man's ingenuity can more or less keep pace with his visions the fulfilment of this dream can be traced right back to 2000 years ago. In 40 BC the concept of a *life annuity* was born with the passing of a Roman law called the *Lex Faludia de legatio.*

This law attempted to prevent any shilly-shallying or misplaced favouritism on the part of a Roman patriarch as to who inherited his property: his *pied à terre* in Rome, his country villa, and his various olive groves and vineyards. Even should there be ructions between father and son – due to the way the latter wore his toga or whatever – the legal heir was to get at least a quarter of the legacies. In order to evaluate this sum the legacies were regarded as yearly payments for life and a scale of values was drawn up.

Once this scale of values had been established it was not long before it was put to use in a rather different practice – the bestowing of a pre-calculated sum of money each year upon a beneficiary known as an annuitant. Unfortunately this new arrangement was not totally flawless. In order to be on the receiving end of the pre-arranged yearly income the

annuitant was required first of all to hand over a substantial capital sum.

Did this not rather defeat the purpose of the whole transaction? What was the point in handing over your money, merely to get it back in annual instalments?

To be perfectly honest, there was absolutely no point in purchasing an annuity if you weren't going to live long enough to recoup through your yearly income more money than you actually parted with in the first place. However, if you happened to survive to an unexpectedly ripe old age, the chances were that you'd gradually rake in a substantial profit.

In other words, both the annuity seller and the annuitant stood a chance of gaining from the deal. Which party came out on top depended almost entirely on the longevity of the latter.

As the centuries passed and annuity fever spread throughout Europe, a few unscrupulous citizens inevitably glimpsed in this financial gamble an opportunity for wealth beyond measure. By advertising extraordinarily generous annuity rates in return for ridiculously low capital outlays they attracted hordes of gullible investors and pocketed their cash. At this juncture the relatively God-fearing promptly vanished. Their more sinister colleagues applied the vanishing trick to their 'troublesome' clients. In 1350 the town of Brunswick actually had to stop private individuals from granting annuities as the mysterious disappearances of relatively long-lived – and thus expensive – annuitants could no longer be overlooked.

England's most infamous annuity-monger was the evocatively nicknamed 'Vulture' Hopkins who dabbled prosperously in fraud, bribery, perjury and surreptitious strangulation.

Of course the chicanery of the pedlar was not altogether unmatched by the chicanery of the buyer, and even 'Vulture' Hopkins could occasionally be taken in by a last-minute substitution of a hale and hearty octagenarian for a newly deceased annuitant. In fact if you could rely on your friends, avoid back-alleys at all times and tolerate your ulcers and insomnia, you could grow as rich as you grew old.

Readers with weak constitutions will be relieved to learn that life annuities have come a long way since those early rumbustious days. They have developed from a wild financial risk into an attractive investment proposition – and that's not merely due to the fact that modern annuitants need no longer fear for their lives. Today's annuities, sold by insurance companies rather than individuals, are based on a sound financial and actuarial structure, and provide a high return because they are bought with an increasingly valuable commodity, the capital sum.

Unfortunately there are not that many of us nowadays who can boast a capital sum lying around, doing nothing in particular, which could be put to no better use than the purchase of an annuity. The exceptions are those people who, towards the end of their working lives or at retirement itself, have accumulated a nest-egg which must see them through their remaining years.

In fact the onset of retirement is both the ideal and the most popular time to invest in an annuity. Not only will the annuitant be spared the headache of confining himself to an inadequate annual budget, he will avoid the disastrous consequences of outliving his savings. Safe in this knowledge he could be relaxed enough to go on living for ages and collect a handsome profit into the bargain. In fact, statistics show that annuitants tend to live appreciably longer than the norm.

Where does all this leave the younger self-employed man or woman, still hard at work and with no more than a current income to invest, but still dreaming that dream of a regular annual bonanza?

Man's ingenuity actually had a bit of a struggle to keep pace with this particular vision.

4 Annuities on the never-never

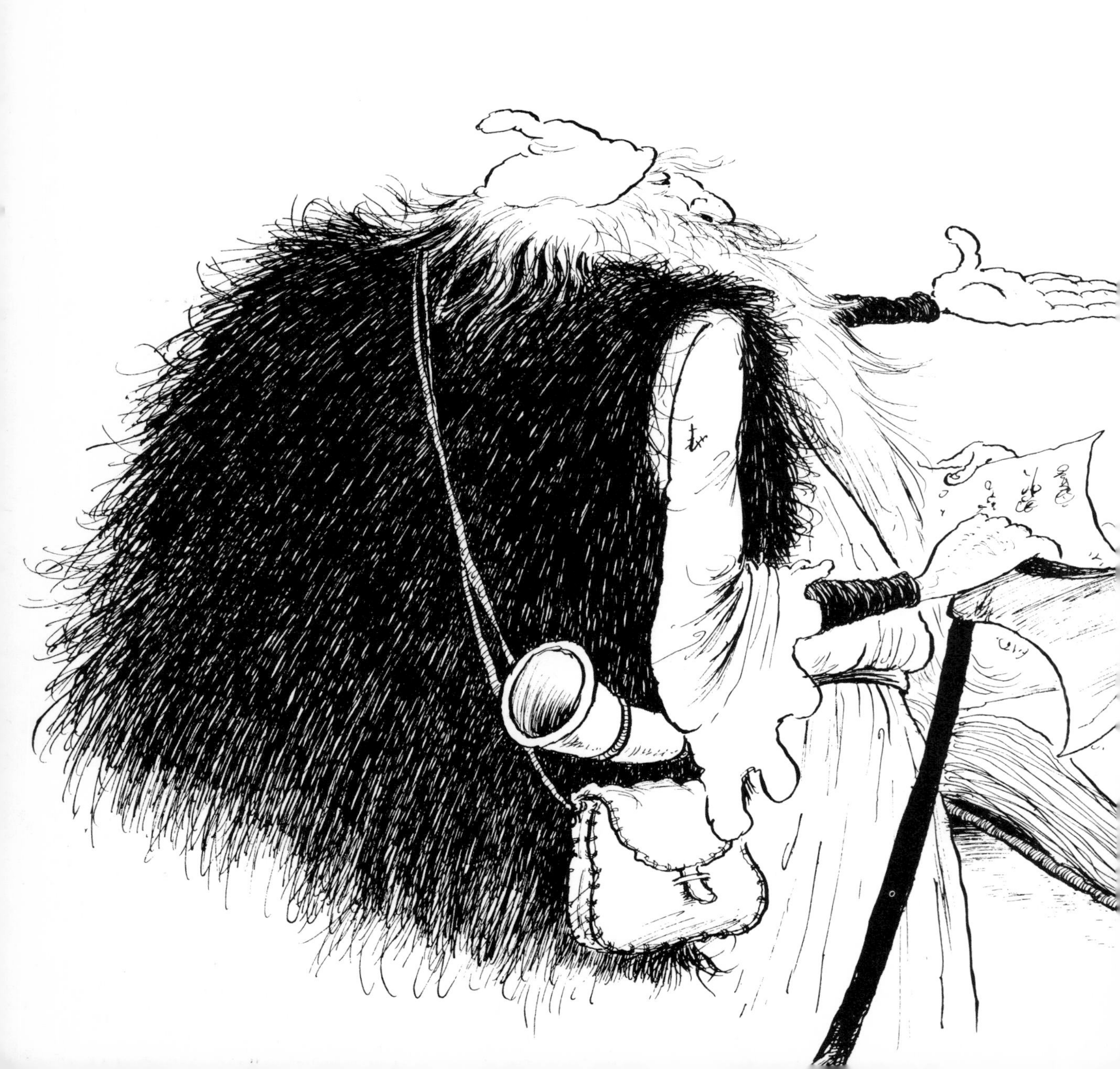

If you can't put down cash for your new car or house you can always buy it on the never-never. With hire purchase and leasing you may speed away in your Porsche, although theoretically you own no more than its chassis. With an endowment or repayment mortgage you may sprawl all over your semi although strictly speaking only the scullery is yours.

In very much the same way, if the self-employed can't put down cash for a life annuity they can now buy one on the never-never. The only difference is that they may not drive off in it, inhabit it, or otherwise enjoy its advantages until they've completed their series of payments.

The official name for this arrangement is a *deferred annuity*. Laymen could call it a pension scheme.

The concept of a deferred annuity has been around for a good while longer than either hire purchase or mortgages. Unfortunately the translation of concept into fair and feasible scheme has been fraught with blunder – for obvious reasons. Just put yourself in the place of a medieval Town Councillor with instructions to raise capital for urgent municipal building projects by granting annuities to local citizens.

Providing each citizen has the specified sum of money in his pouch you'll probably offer him the same annuity deal whether he's 28 or 88. We know that even as late as the seventeenth century the Dutch government was selling annuities irrespective of the applicants' ages.

Although in hindsight this seems a procedure doomed to disaster – you could soon be paying out to your younger annuitants whatever profit you might make on the elderly – you don't worry too much about it at the time. Raising the necessary cash is of paramount importance now. Who knows: in ten years' time the municipal income accruing from the completed building works may be sufficient to stretch to life annuities for every man, woman and child in town.

But how would you react to a fairly respectable group of shopkeepers, scribes and alchemists, with not much more than a groat between them (business and base metal not being what they used to be) and a preposterous proposal to buy their way into your annuity scheme by instalments? Indeed, by individually calculated annual instalments based on each man's present age and the number of years to go before he reaches his chosen retirement age?

In order to ensure that the scheme was viable for your side as well as theirs two important skills, not even in their infancy at the time, would need to be brought into play: the first, probability and risk mathematics; the second, long-term investment know-how.

It was not until the seventeenth century that the first skill really got off the ground. Its inventor was the French mathematician and philosopher Blaise Pascal.

Pascal's neighbours in the early 1650s were a pretty sceptical bunch. All right, so Blaise had proved himself to be the leading expert on such esoteric matters as the geometry of conics and the infinitesimal calculus, but no one was going to tell them that his current 'experiments' with dice and playing-cards would further advance the frontiers of mathematical knowledge.

In fact, Pascal's theory of probability arising from these experiments, used in conjunction with the rather limited information on longevity and mortality available at the time, proved the basis for the scientifically calculated, equitable state of deferred annuities as we know them today.

It also provided his fellow countryman and celebrated mathematician Abraham de Moivre with a splendid opportunity to set himself up as a gamblers' odds-maker in the coffee-houses of the City of London. Here he advised punters on such matters as 'the probability of throwing an Ace in three throws of the dice,' or 'how many Tickets should be taken in a Lottery' to produce an even chance of winning a big prize.

The second skill took even longer to get under way.

In the Middle Ages various artisans banded together for mutual security in associations known as craft guilds. These operated a sort of all-embracing benefit scheme: the idea being that in return for a small regular contribution each member could make sure of financial support in old age and adversity.

Unfortunately the money remained locked up in a big chest until such time as it was needed. Because it didn't increase in value there was quite often not enough to go round when payment fell due. Contributors were forced to chip in the extra.

Of course inflation such as we know it today didn't really exist in medieval times. But that's not to say that prices remained stable over the years. For example, between the Norman Conquest of 1066 and the accession of Edward III in 1327 the price of wheat varied from 8d. to £6 8s. a quarter, reaching its highest figure in 1270. At that time a farm labourer was earning a maximum of a penny a day during harvest time and an artisan couldn't have been doing much better. The need for secure investment growth in any long-term financial scheme to off-set the erosion caused by spiralling prices, as well as to rectify possible initial under-funding, became increasingly apparent. Nor was the fact overlooked that such growth would reduce the price of contributions and turn some rather haphazard projects into most attractive cost-effective propositions.

If you can visualize small groups of enthusiastic amateurs trying their hand at investment you can understand why the process has taken so long to get right. Even nowadays investment expertise, though at a very high level, cannot guarantee success: so much still depends on luck.

However, with the gradual coming together of the two new skills – risk mathematics and long-term employment of capital – deferred annuity schemes started to attract the attention they deserved, primarily among employers wishing to provide pensions for their employees. The self-employed had still to wait for the arrival of Tucker and his men.

5 The triple triumph of Mr Tucker

James Millard Tucker KC was the Chairman of a committee of six set up in August 1950 to investigate private and occupational savings schemes. The recommendations in one section of his report, laid before Parliament in February 1954, were the most exciting and advantageous propositions ever to be made on behalf of the self-employed investor. So revolutionary were they, in fact, that some of them had to be swept hurriedly under the carpet, where they remained for nearly two decades.

Since enlightened legislation has at last rescued and vindicated them, all Tucker's tax treats can now be revealed.

Every self-employed person in pre-Tucker times saw taxation as Public Enemy Number One, pouncing on both business and investment profits like some indiscriminate Chicago mobster. What Tucker proposed was the setting-up of three well-policed zones affording protection against the ravages of tax and enabling self-employed pension schemes to flourish and multiply.

The first tax-free zone defended contributions. Tucker recommended that full income and surtax relief should be given on all premiums paid into self-employed deferred annuity schemes, provided each scheme member's annual premium did not exceed a certain percentage of his annual earnings. The suggested percentage was as high as twelve per cent in some cases.

The second zone safeguarded the money as it grew. Tucker urged that the funds into which the premiums would be paid should be fully exempt from tax.

SELF-EMPLOYED

The third zone protected the proceeds of the scheme. Tucker suggested that part of the eventual pension should be payable in the form of a tax-free lump sum – up to a maximum figure of £10,000. The rest should be taxed at the relatively low rate applicable to earned income.

With the exception of a few minor details, Tucker's proposals have since become law. As a result self-employed deferred annuities – commonly known as *self-employed retirement annuities* or *personal pension plans* – are head and shoulders above any other retirement savings scheme available to the self-employed. There is quite simply no other granary like this one.

However personal pension plans have become so justifiably popular that the insurance companies and life offices that sell them have diversified them a little. There are now three main types of scheme – *non-profit, with-profits* and *deposit administration**, and *unit-linked** – all offering almost identical tax concessions but varying in other respects to cover the whole range of private investment requirements.

Before we look at these variations in detail it's worth noting some rather surprising facts about self-employed retirement annuities in general.

Firstly, they are open to anyone who is not a member of an occupational pension scheme – including business partners and company directors – or to anyone who has two sources of income, one of which doesn't carry pension rights –

* These schemes have evolved from deferred annuities although they are not true deferred annuities themselves. See Chapters 6 and 7.

including occasional earnings from such activities as writing, lecturing or consultancy work. In other words, you don't necessarily have to be self-employed to qualify.

Secondly, over two hundred separate schemes are currently being offered by over one hundred separate insurance companies and life offices, but to get the policy that best suits your circumstances you need make only one appointment — with your insurance broker. That's not to stop you doing your own shopping around if you should so wish, although it's important to bear in mind that some pension policies are only obtainable through brokers. If you'd like to use the services of a broker, but don't know where to find one, you can ask the British Insurance Brokers' Association* to recommend one in your area.

Lastly, and most importantly, Tucker's trail-blazing tax concessions, once considered inordinately far-reaching, have actually proved the inspiration for a new generation of even further-reaching tax advantages. Personal pension policy-holders can now make use of such marvels as their 'carry forward' and 'carry back' provisions†; those providing for their dependants can also do so on very favourable tax terms.

Self-employed retirement annuities were once considered the poor relatives of highly graced and favoured occupational pension schemes. Because one man stuck his neck out, they can now hold their heads up to their former betters.

* See the address list at the back of the book.

† See Chapter 9.

6 Penny plain and tuppence coloured

A *non-profit* personal pension is the cheapest you can buy. Yet in return for your modest premiums your company will guarantee you a minimum yearly income at retirement, payable for the rest of your life.

So what's the catch?

The answer is that any sum of money remaining static over a longish period of time will be chewed to pieces by inflation and prove to be a hopeless investment. That's why so few of these policies are sold.

Nevertheless there are instances where non-profit schemes really come into their own and where their unchanging amount of pension, allied to their cheapness, proves both handy and efficient.

Say you're a grocer due to retire in around five years' time. You've already saved quite a bit for your future through a life assurance endowment policy,* but you'd like to raise the level of your existing arrangement by a certain specific amount. A non-profit scheme is exactly the answer to your requirements here.

* See Chapter 12.

Several pegs up from non-profit schemes you'll find *with-profits* personal pensions: growing increasingly sophisticated, but always retaining their innate security. With-profits schemes will cost you more than their profitless counterparts, but will in most cases prove much superior to them. The extra amount of premium you pay out will buy you a stake in the tax-free investment profits of your company, over and above the minimum pension guaranteed to you.

This slice of the action comes to you as a series of *reversionary bonuses,* tacked onto your basic minimum pension, usually once every three years. Although the amount of each bonus reflects in general terms how well your

company's investments are doing, you won't normally go without a bonus even in a crisis slump time – your company will scrape the bottom of its reserve barrel if necessary to see you're not short-changed.

Once bonuses have been added to your pension they can't be taken away, so the result is a steady, secure increase of your guaranteed minimum over the years.

In addition to reversionary bonuses some companies offer a *final, terminal* or *vesting* bonus just prior to retirement. This reflects any surplus of investment profits not yet credited to you, and sometimes allows for recently improved annuity rates. A few companies will even continue to add bonuses after your pension starts to be paid, although these normally finish their job when you finish yours.

A tiny minority of life offices calculate their with-profits policies in a slightly different way and call them *deposit administration* policies. Although there is a subtle difference, from a company's point of view, between a with-profits and a deposit administration scheme, they are to all intents and purposes one and the same thing to the investor, providing him with similar value for money.

No company can say for sure what bonus rates they will pay out in the future to with-profits or deposit administration policy-holders, but they all make a point of quoting estimated bonuses and probable pension amounts, largely based on current trends and results. Although you should accept these for just what they are – estimates – you'll find that past performance is not at all a misleading means of evaluating future potential.

Reversionary bonus rates, as we've seen, have rock-like qualities: steady and secure, they tend to change very gradually. In addition companies with a good track record are particularly proud of their competitive position and make every effort to keep it up. Thus, despite the fact that different types of bonus make comparison awkward, a quick sift through various companies' previous records should give you a fair idea of what to expect in the years to come.

It's worth noting here that once you commit yourself to a personal pension by paying your first premium there's no going back. From this point on you lose full control of your savings, as you can only get your money out again in the form of a pension. Under no circumstances can you surrender your policy or assign it to someone else.

Normally, however, you'll have embarked on a pension scheme because you want a pension. Such praiseworthy singleness of purpose incurs no penalty.

7 Snakes and ladders

If the idea of blackjack attracts you, so will a *unit-linked* pension plan. With this kind of scheme you're taking a real gamble on the future success of certain investments: your premium money is tied directly to various units in an investment fund and your pension depends almost entirely on how well they perform.

Those with nerves of iron who can stomach the uncertainty of an unpredictable pension may be encouraged to risk all by two important facts. Firstly they stand to gain as much in the way of income as they may theoretically lose. Indeed, past performance of such pension plans – though no more than an indication of future potential – has yielded highly encouraging results, with growth rates averaging around 10 per cent. Secondly many schemes guarantee to pay out a certain minimum annuity should the South Sea Bubble burst and Wall Street crash again. As recently as 1974 the British stock market collapsed; in early 1975 it showed a giddy 100 per cent rise in a mere six weeks; next time who knows which way the scales will tip?

What exactly happens to your hard-earned premiums? Normally a percentage is deducted to cover your company's charges, and the rest goes towards buying units in a special tax-free investment fund set up by the company. This is usually a fund of different shares, or various types of property, or sometimes a mixture of both.

Look twice at the company that puts your money into an authorized unit trust or an investment trust company: such funds are not fully exempt from capital gains tax, and you may end up paying this indirectly. However if their investment record is particularly good this is unlikely to be a problem.

Theoretically the value of your accumulating units will yo-yo up and down in line with your fund's investments until you retire, at which time you start to receive a pension based on whatever they happen to be worth, and whatever annuity rates happen to be current.

In practice, however, the situation is slightly more complicated than this. First of all, company deductions can be made from the interest on your investment as well as from your premiums, and the extent of these deductions varies tremendously from company to company. For example, extra-large amounts are sometimes deducted from the premiums you pay in the first year or two of your scheme – the most valuable premiums from your point of view – thus ensuring that you get off to a slower start than if charges were spread evenly between premiums paid over several years. In cases where a chunk of the interest on your investment is pocketed by your company, your yo-yo will bounce lower than if this money were re-invested on your behalf. Luckily companies' deductions are usually explained in their relevant brochure; if you read through this carefully you should know just where you stand.

Secondly, some companies offer you a choice of different kinds of fund and the possibility of splitting your premiums between them, switching the various proportions around – at a price – whenever you feel so inclined. Be warned – unless you are an extremely astute investor you will find it fearsomely difficult to boost your pension by subdividing and swopping around in this way. However, you may find that it pays to switch your units from your fluctuating shares-and-property fund to a steady fixed interest or deposit fund, should the market be particularly depressed a couple of years prior to your retirement.

Thirdly, most companies give you the option of keeping your pension linked to your investment even after retirement. In other words, even while it is being paid, your pension could continue to fluctuate with the performance of your units.

Unfortunately it's difficult to say whether it's a good idea to plump for this option or not. It would come in very handy if, say, share prices were low when your pension started: a unit-linked pension would not stay permanently depressed. However, the starting pension under such an arrangement is very low—usually less than half the 'normal' level pension, and of course your units could always go down snakes instead of up ladders....

Finally, since the annuity rates which determine your pension at retirement could be at the mercy of conditions prevalent at the time, few companies will guarantee you more than a very basic minimum rate.

There are a few very general guidelines to follow if you've developed a sudden hankering for a unit-linked personal pension. They won't necessarily keep you afloat should the stock market take a very deep plunge but they're likely to keep you buoyant at all other times.

As with other pension schemes, you should choose—or check that your broker chooses—a policy sold by a long-established, sizable life assurance company which is a member of the Life Offices' Association* or the Associated Scottish Life Offices.*

Look carefully at the company's explanation of its charges and work out how much of your premium money and investment interest will be lost to you.

See what guarantees are incorporated into the policy and whether they're worth the paper they're printed on.

Consider a company's current investment performance and its general all-round investment record.

If you're not fully satisfied, try several other policies from several other companies....

Most importantly, unless your hankering brooks no restraint, don't put all your eggs in one basket: take out a unit-linked policy alongside a with-profits plan and hope to get the best of both worlds.

After all, when you're dicing with your future livelihood you can't afford to take too many chances.

* See the address list at the back of the book.

8 As ye sow, so shall ye reap

One of the major advantages of personal pension schemes is their tremendous flexibility. Like a suit in umpteen possible sizes they vary extensively enough to mould themselves snugly around you, whatever your particular circumstances and pension requirements. As with a suit cut during your working life but not worn until your retirement, a considerable amount of measuring takes place at the outset of your scheme – and quite a lot of altering and re-shaping at its termination, when you discover you've changed shape over the years . . . .

The income of most self-employed people tends to be irregular, fluctuating as it often does according to the whims of customers or market trends. Steady monthly pension premiums in these instances are often inappropriate, proving either untimely and too high or inadequate and not sufficiently concentrated.

Most companies will allow you to humour your pocket by varying your premiums from year to year. 'Regular' premiums can in fact fluctuate between the Inland Revenue's upper limit* and a company's own lower limit: usually £100 a year. The best thing to do is to select a basic premium that you know you'll be able to pay regularly, and top it up whenever your profits permit, either with an additional contribution or with a series of completely separate single premiums.

A *single premium policy* is a very valuable option which can stand on its own as conveniently as it can supplement a regular premium arrangement. What happens is that you contract to pay just one premium at a time, so you can alter

* See Chapter 9.

the amount you contribute each year without any difficulty at all. Amazingly enough, you can actually postpone payment of each separate premium until the end of the relevant tax year, when you'll know exactly what your financial position is. Indeed, within certain generous limits, you can even backdate your payment.* What's more, you'll find that company charges are usually lower for single premium policy-holders, and in addition you'll be able to spread your risk between different companies and different types of policy. In fact the only real drawback with a single premium scheme is the bother of having to fill out a fresh proposal form every year.

For those committed to regular premiums, varying or not, the biggest worry is the complete inability one year to pay any sort of premium at all. Luckily most companies allow a certain amount of elasticity in this situation too. In a very bad year you could miss one premium without them coming down on you like a ton of bricks. They may permit you to pay up a month or two later, or let you off altogether, provided you agree to accept a slightly reduced pension.

However enough is enough and you won't be allowed a repeat non-performance. Should you be unfortunate enough to have a second terrible year, your policy will normally be made *paid-up* — in other words, frozen until your retirement, at which time you'll receive a smaller pension than originally planned. You should make sure that the basis for calculating the paid-up value of your pension is guaranteed in your policy: it should be roughly proportionate to the premiums paid. Bonuses, if applicable, should continue to be added as usual.

* See Chapter 9.

The vast majority of companies allow you the greatest possible freedom when it comes to choosing your retirement age: the time you'll want your pension to start being paid. Right at the outset of your scheme you may have to name a date, but normally you'll be able to retire with very little notice at any time between your sixtieth and your seventy-fifth birthday. The older you are when you retire, the bigger your pension will be.

Certain categories of people are in fact permitted to retire at a rather earlier age than most. Jockeys, racing drivers, boxers, wrestlers and footballers can claim their pensions from the age of 50; pilots, distant-water trawler skippers, female nurses, midwives, health visitors and physiotherapists have to wait another five years. Those incapacitated by accident or ill-health, whatever their former profession, may also be allowed an early retirement.

In order to draw your pension you don't have to stop work. Indeed some enlightened life offices, realizing that a sudden switch from job to no job and from earned income to pension can cause all sorts of disruptions, have dreamt up a way of alleviating the transition. This is known as *partial retirement.*

A partial retirement option is a boon for anyone in his sixties who wants to withdraw gradually from his work, such as a grocer starting to hand the reins of his business over to his son, or a solicitor choosing to remain with his firm on a diminishing part-time basis.

What he does is draw part of his pension straight away to maintain his level of income, and continue to pay reduced premiums. As he cuts back on his work, say in three easy stages, he draws proportionately more of his pension until he finally retires altogether with the full remaining amount.

This result can be achieved by having several pension policies, as he could start drawing the first at the age of 60 and the rest at, say, three- or five-yearly intervals right up to 75.

Whenever you make your decision about how and when you want to retire, you will also have to consider how and, significantly, by whom you want your pension paid.

Because of a recent change in the law, you may either accept the annuity that your company has arranged to pay you, or you may ask them to transfer its cash equivalent to another company offering a better annuity rate, and draw a higher pension from them. This *untied cash option* is an innovation which can be put to most profitable use, provided you do some research into comparative annuity rates or pay a return visit to your broker.

Your original company won't penalize you severely for taking your money and running, but it may charge a small sum. This should not detract from the overriding advantage of the operation: a personal pension policy-holder can now reap the financial benefits of both a good investment company and a company with good annuity rates.

As for how your pension will be paid, the choice is as long as your arm. However, all companies allow you one especially valuable option that you should, whatever your circumstances, make full use of: the exchange or 'commutation' of part of your taxable pension for a *tax-free cash sum.*

This tax-free sum, which must not exceed three times your remaining yearly pension, is important as extra capital, and doubly important as it can be used to buy a tax-favoured annuity to supplement your pension.*

Once you've plumped for the cash you can choose to have your remaining pension paid to you every month, every quarter or every year if you prefer.

Some companies now offer you the choice of an income that remains fixed throughout your retirement, or one that

* See Chapter 9.

starts at a lower rate but increases steadily year by year. This arrangement, strictly for those with confidence in their longevity, is usually known as an *escalating* pension. A very few companies offer a *dynamic* pension: like the escalating one this starts at a lower level, but because it continues to share in profits after it starts to be paid it should give better value for money.

To spite fate you can even decide on a lower pension to be paid out for a guaranteed minimum of five or even ten years, whether you're around to receive it or not. More rationally you could forgo part of your pension to provide an income for your wife, should she outlive you.

All in all, if variety is the spice of life, the self-employed are in for a fairly piquant eve of retirement.

9 Quadruple your money

How would you like to save £3000 a year at a net cost of only £750? You could with a personal pension scheme. If your annual income is £20,000 and you're paying 75 per cent tax on part of it, the Inland Revenue will be happy to subsidize your savings to the tune of £2250!

However, it's not only the well-off who benefit from the Inland Revenue's benevolence towards prospective pensioners. Every personal pension policy-holder can receive full income tax relief on all his premiums—whether single, regular or varying—at his highest rate of tax paid. Even those of us on mere basic rate tax, currently 33 per cent, will normally receive a gift-wrapped £33 for every £100 we put aside.

Tax concessions abound right the way through the personal pension process. Your premiums will normally go into a special pension fund whose income and capital gains are entirely tax-free. Your pension at retirement will be taxable, but at the lower rate of earned income rather than as investment income. As we've seen, the cash sum you can choose to take at retirement is completely free of tax and could be used to purchase a tax-favoured immediate annuity. Only the interest part of an immediate annuity is taxable: the remainder, which is considered to be repayment of capital, is tax-free. Although the interest part is taxable as investment income and may therefore be subject to a surcharge, it could still pay you to plump for pension plus lump sum/annuity rather than pension all on its own.

Personal pension premiums being particularly favoured by the tax-man, however, it's worth exploring the concessions made to them in considerable detail.

The highest amount of annual premium for which full tax relief is currently permitted is stipulated by the Inland Revenue as 15 per cent of each individual's own 'net relevant earnings' for the year, or £3000, whichever is less. In plain English 'net relevant earnings' means your non-pensionable earnings less certain deductions—such as agreed business losses and capital allowances, expenses and mortgage interest which you can't offset against any other income.

As you can see from the example already given, these upper limits are far from niggardly. For those born before 1916 but still contributing merrily they are even less so—these stalwart oldsters are allowed full tax relief on an even greater proportion of their net relevant earnings, or up to an even higher monetary limit.

What's more, if any self-employed person's total contributions exceed the 15 per cent limit one year, but drop below it the next, he can carry the first year's excess forward to benefit from the second year's shortfall. In other words, he can pay in a premium that's over his 15 per cent limit, get tax relief on the 15 per cent part of it immediately, and tax relief on what remains by going under his limit in subsequent years. Provided he doesn't pay more than the £3000 in any one year, he can *carry forward* any percentage surplus almost indefinitely and exploit his percentage allowance to the full.

This procedure is an absolute boon for, say, a none-too-prosperous but highly pension-conscious window-cleaner whose net relevant earnings total £4000. The Revenue rules would let him pay £600 worth of premium a year, but he can't afford so much and is actually contributing only £300 to his with-profits scheme.

One day, much to his surprise, he learns that the old dear at number 22 has gone and left him £5000. If he has his wits about him he will slap £3000 of this into his policy as soon as his premium becomes due, and the remaining £2000 a year later.

If we suppose that his income and subsequent premiums remain steady, he will continue to be eligible for tax relief on £600 a year. He can continue to claim half his relief on his normal premiums and he can use the other half over the years to offset regular chunks of his unexpected inheritance against his tax.

The windfall that reduces your tax bill as it grows to support you in your old age is some windfall indeed.

He may manage to set the full £5000 against tax before he retires, but even if he doesn't it won't bother him much. He can still take his maximum tax-free cash sum at retirement; all that happens is that the part of his remaining pension which can be attributed to the not-yet-tax-relieved premiums will be taxable as investment income rather than earned income.

Amazingly enough, that same window-cleaner can *carry back* his provision almost as profitably as he can carry it forward. Any self-employed person who didn't or couldn't take full advantage of tax relief available to him in past years may put aside single premiums and have these set off against earlier years' assessments.

He must pay the additional contributions and notify the Inland Revenue that he has done so either before the relevant tax years' assessments have been made or within 6 months of their becoming final.

However, it may be possible to re-open one's finalized assessment for a fairly trivial reason, such as the trip you made to the Midlothian Trade Fair six years ago which you quite forgot to claim. While you're haggling over your bus fare you could just slip in an extra single premium . . .

It's worth noting here that three situations will serve to reduce your maximum tax relief allowance. If you have two jobs,* one of which carries pension rights, you will find that the monetary ceiling of £3000 will be reduced by 15 per cent of your pensionable earnings. Any additional premiums you may pay to provide for your dependants† will also come out of your allowance: these payments must not exceed 5 per cent of your net relevant earnings, or a maximum of £1000. Finally any extra premium you put towards a disability premium waiver option* will once again have to come within your allowance.

Tax relief is not automatically obtainable: it has to be claimed through a document known as a *Self-Employed Premium Certificate* or SEPC. This certificate is issued to every policy-holder at the outset of his scheme, and he should send it to his tax office the first time he requests relief.

When will he get his relief? That depends on which tax schedule he comes under. For directors and employees taxed under Schedule E, tax relief is normally available against earnings in the same tax year in which contributions are paid. However, the self-employed and partners taxed under Schedule D are usually assessed for tax in the tax year following their accounting year.

Should this state of affairs not be to their liking they can always write a humble letter to the Inspector of Taxes asking for relief to be given against earnings for a year or accounting period ending before contributions are made.

* See Chapter 11.

†See Chapter 10.

The go-ahead will generally be given, provided that contributions are made within that afore-mentioned six-month period after the relevant assessment becomes final.

The only tax obstacle left to demolish is capital transfer tax. This is a tax imposed when capital totalling over £25,000 changes hands by way of gift or on death.

Should you die prematurely, certain benefits which could arise from your pension policy would potentially be liable to capital transfer tax in your estate, provided this topped the £25,000 mark. (For this purpose your estate may include large gifts made in the past.) Fortunately you can almost always protect your dependants' interests in this matter without much difficulty at all.

You could for example make sure that any proceeds from your policy will go to your wife or husband as there is no capital transfer tax payable on estate transfer between spouses.

Alternatively you could arrange for any cash sum payable at your death* to be converted into an annuity of some sort as, unlike a cash sum, an annuity would be free of this tax.

Finally you should try to avoid the pension payment option that guarantees you a pension for a minimum five or ten years, unless you have little faith in your longevity. For if you die during your guarantee period the remaining income will not only be liable to capital transfer tax, it will also be taxable as investment income. And you'll have had a less good pension deal into the bargain....

* See Chapter 10.

10 'These are the children That go with the wife That goes with the house that Jack built'

As you gradually accumulate your substantial retirement nest-egg, the idea of dying before being able to lay hands on it will quite rightly be far from your mind. After all, if you're dead and buried it won't matter one way or the other what happens to your carefully amassed savings – you'll certainly not be able to spend them in whatever Celestial Shopping Centre may be found beyond the Pearly Gates.

However, if in this eventuality you should leave behind a wife and children – or other dependants – spare a thought for what this money could mean to them.

What normally happens when a policy-holder dies before retirement is that his gross premiums are returned to his estate or dependants, either as a lump sum (possibly liable to capital transfer tax*) or, provided the amount is substantial, in the form of a pension (not liable to capital transfer tax) payable to his widow or other nominee. Very frequently the sum includes compound interest at around 4 to 6 per cent per annum—or in one instance 10 per cent; occasionally accumulated bonuses are added instead. In the case of unit-linked schemes the refund usually equals the current value of the investments.

It is nevertheless not unknown for absolutely nothing to be paid back at all: some schemes provide slightly more in the way of pension by cancelling any kind of pre-retirement death benefit.

What all this boils down to is that a policy-holder's dependants may get very little out of his savings. At the very best, with the 10 per cent scheme, they'll get a most reasonable return on his money should he die just before he's due to start drawing his pension. At the very worst they'll be left without a penny.

Of course a free-wheeling bachelor may not care two hoots about this state of affairs. Nor will a prospective pensioner who has taken out a separate life assurance policy to protect his family against his untimely end. Anyone else may well care to consider a life assurance *term* policy written into the body of his pension scheme itself.

A personal pension scheme incorporating term assurance family protection obviously costs more than the 'ordinary'

* See Chapter 9.

version, although the extra payment is actually limited by the Inland Revenue for tax concession reasons. It may not exceed 5 per cent of the policy-holder's net relevant earnings or a maximum of £1000, and it must come within his total annual pension premium allowance. Within these confines it attracts full tax relief at his highest tax rate.

What this means in effect is that our £20,000-a-year example could contribute an annual £1000 to safeguard his family at a net cost of only £250. What does his family stand to gain? Three alternative types of benefit could be provided by his extra premiums.

The first is a pre-agreed cash sum (possibly liable to capital transfer tax*) which will be paid out only if his death occurs before his retirement.

The second is a pension for his widow (taxable as earned income but not liable to capital transfer tax*) payable should he die before her, either before or after his retirement.

The third alternative is a regular tax-free income payable once every quarter to his family should he die within a certain period of time. The income would continue right up to the end of this term, but then cease.

It's important to note that you may need to provide medical evidence of your good health before you can arrange this sort of extra protection for your family.

These three benefits are concerned mainly with family provision if death occurs before retirement; subsequent family protection measures can always be taken at retirement itself. However, those already committed to pension policies

* See Chapter 9.

which overlook the possibility of early death can relax: it's never too late to fill this particular protection gap, provided you're medically sound.

The simple remedy is a separate term assurance policy, available from many life offices. Take one out now to last you until your retirement — or up to the age of 75 – and you'll never need to spend another sleepless night wondering how on earth your family will cope without you. Fortunately, even your separate term assurance premiums will normally be allowed full tax relief at your highest rate.

Should you for any reason wish to combine a ten-year-minimum retirement savings plan with full family protection right up to your retirement, putting the emphasis more on unlimited savings than maximum tax concessions, a life assurance *endowment** *with-profits* or *unit-linked* policy could perhaps prove preferable to a personal pension plan.

Providing for your wife and family after your retirement is generally a very straightforward matter. The only thing that may possibly confuse you is that different names and conditions have been dreamt up for what is essentially the same basic idea: you forgo part of your pension so that when you die your widow (or other dependant) gets one of her — or his — own.

Your particular scheme may call this arrangement a *widow's continuing pension* option, or a *joint life and survivor* option applicable to widowers as well as widows; it matters little. What you will practically always end up doing is exchanging part of your pension to provide an income for your spouse.

* See Chapter 12.

Say a man at 65 is entitled through his self-employed scheme to a pension of £6974 a year (just to get out of the unrealistic habit of using nice round figures). Faithful to the last he'll do without a smallish chunk of this, say £1649, to make sure of keeping his widow in the style to which she was accustomed. His pension after this deduction works out at £5325. And this same £5325 is what his widow can look forward to every year for the rest of her life. In some schemes the surviving spouse might receive slightly less than they were both getting before.

Making provision for your family of course shouldn't stop you from trying to outdo Methuselah: he completely flummoxed his pension company by living to the ripe old age of 969.

JOB SHEET
CLOSING DOWN

11 Look before you leap

Self-employment is a somewhat precarious way of life: highly gratifying inasmuch as your successes are the fruit of your own brain sauce and elbow grease; infuriating insofar as the buck of your failures rests squarely with you. The responsibility for 'keeping at it' is enormous, and many a diligent candlestick-maker longs for the tranquil security of a cushy office job or the sudden intervention of fate.

The trouble is, any desertion of the self-employed post could wreak havoc on your personal pension scheme and therefore on your future.

Let's say that after eight years or so in a scheme you closed your shop and went to work for an employer. Your insurance company will normally make your policy *paid-up*. In other words, you will stop paying premiums but will still be entitled to a certain amount of pension at retirement: the *paid-up value* of your policy.

Although most companies will make sure you get reasonable paid-up value for your money, some may penalize you for abandoning them. Even if you cannot yet envisage setting off for pastures new, it is therefore very important to check that, at least after two or three years, your particular paid-up value would be roughly proportionate to the amount of premiums you'd have paid. See whether bonuses would continue to be added as usual in a with-profits or deposit administration scheme, and whether your units would carry on growing in a unit-linked plan. This is the only way you can make sure of getting your just personal pension deserts.

Some people may be encouraged to note that those who switch from a self-employed to an occupational pension scheme fairly early on in their working life are likely to do pretty well for themselves at retirement. It is a sad fact that since self-employed pensions are dependent on — and therefore limited by — the earnings of the self-employed throughout their career, they can never quite catch up with the advantages of an occupational 'final pay' scheme, particularly when it comes to grappling with inflation. Unfortunately in the early years of a personal scheme there tends to be a shortage of cash to spend on premiums. Later on, when large amounts of spare money are looking for a home, Inland Revenue cash limits clamp down on compensatory over-spending.

Of course, leaving a personal scheme of one's own free will and for some chosen and very viable alternative is one thing; the intervention of fate could well be another.

The self-employed, whatever their pension situation, normally cannot afford to be out of work through ill-health for more than a short period. Prolonged sickness in these circumstances is something to be feared; disability something to be dreaded. Savings or unearned income of some kind may tide them over the worst of a temporary incapacity but won't last indefinitely.

Imagine how much more serious the whole business of ill-health becomes when a pension is involved as well. Even if the victim has some unearned income to his name he won't be able to pay his pension premiums with it as it won't constitute net relevant earnings. There will be nothing to prevail against the last resort of a paid-up policy with possible penalty. Nothing, that is, except a *disability option*.

In return for a small additional contribution a few companies will agree to waive your pension contributions, should you be forced through accident or sickness to be off work for longer than three months. In other words, your company will undertake to pay your premiums for you so that your suffering won't be increased by loss of pension.

To qualify for a disability option you must be no older than 50 (your cover automatically ceases at 60), your health and occupation must be deemed satisfactory, and your inclusive premium must be somewhere between £100 and £3000 per annum. Single premium policy-holders are not eligible.

Provided they come out of your total premium allowance your additional disability premiums will be granted full tax relief as part of your pension package.

Presumably a 59-year-old escapologist with cardiac symptoms and a hernia could come up against a certain amount of opposition to his request for a disability option—but then they say Houdini could extricate himself from any situation to enjoy the fruits of his labour.

It's worth mentioning here that those with two jobs, only one of which carries pension rights, have a major

incentive to provide themselves with a 'second' pension: the Inland Revenue's cut-back* on their maximum premium payable doesn't affect them adversely at all unless their total earnings exceed £20,000 in any one year.

If you're an accounts clerk in a big firm from 9 a.m. to 5 p.m. and a dance-hall musician from 9 p.m. to all hours, you could top up your occupational pension with a retirement annuity based on your night-time earnings. This way you'd make sure that more of your extra money goes to you, rather than to the tax-man, and at retirement you could really have a ball. Not only would you get a pension, or cash sum plus pension, from your employer, you'd end up with an extra lump sum and income from your nocturnal employment.

* See page 62.

12 'I support myself in a way I am accustomed to live and I tell you, dolling, I can barely afford myself'

(Zsa Zsa Gabor)

A personal pension plan will give you better value for your money than any other retirement savings scheme currently available. But like a banquet for gourmets without the Alka-Seltzer, it's not absolutely perfect.

You lose touch with your savings when you pay your first personal pension premium. Under no circumstances will you see that money again before you reach retirement age.

Inland Revenue restrictions will stop you from investing as much as you might like to. Protection for your family or for yourself will further limit your investment.

Your policy has no cash value right up to the end of its term. No bank or insurance company will ever accept it as security for a loan.

It is therefore not surprising that many personal pension policy-holders welcome a life assurance *endowment* policy with the same sort of appreciation as a *bon viveur* welcomes his Eno's.

An endowment policy is a ten-year minimum savings scheme which bears a passing resemblance to a self-employed retirement annuity.

Just like a prospective pensioner, an endowment policy-holder pays premiums into an investment fund over a pre-arranged period of time, and when this term is up receives his money back with what he hopes will be a satisfactory investment return. Just like a prospective pensioner's, his scheme can be non-profit, with-profits or unit-linked.

However, unlike his counterpart, should he die before his term is up his family will get at the very least a pre-arranged sum of money, known as the *sum assured,* to help them cope with their financial loss.

Furthermore, he will be able to invest as much as he wants in his scheme. After two or three years he'll be able to

use his policy as security for a loan. And if he needs money before his term is up he can 'surrender' or cash in his policy, though he may not get all his premiums back unless he surrenders during the latter part of the term.

Indeed, the only unfortunate aspect of an endowment policy — the sting in the tail of those fruit salts — is that its tax concessions come nowhere near those of a personal pension plan.

An endowment policy-holder can get only 17½ per cent tax relief on that portion of his yearly premium which constitutes less than one-sixth of his annual income or a monetary ceiling of £1500, whichever is greater. Any premium topping these limits is not eligible for tax relief at all.

Worse, the investment fund into which his premiums go will be liable to tax on its investment profits, and will therefore not grow so fast as a comparable pension fund. To compensate partially for this the eventual proceeds of his policy will be payable as a 100 per cent cash sum, entirely free of all tax.

It is important to note that an endowment policy may be taken out by an adult at any stage in his life and for any length of time exceeding ten years. Such a policy is therefore not specifically designed to mature at the policy-holder's retirement age, although many do. Neither need it form a back-up to any other savings or pension scheme, although once again it often does. A three-fold example may serve to enlighten.

The Gibsons love good food. Patrick, 57 and a restaurant guide inspector, occasionally discovers it amidst the limp avocado-with-prawns and the tough minute steaks that are his daily fare and pay his bread and butter. Wife Jacqueline prepares it with gusto at home and abroad: her natural talents are in considerable demand at local functions and she regularly succumbs to persuasion and bribery. Son Alan, at 24 a budding restaurateur, has already made culinary tracks the hard way, progressing from washer-up to sous-chef at the Grand in less than seven years. All three of the Gibsons are endowment policy-holders.

Alan took out his with-profits policy four years ago when he married Pam from the wine bar for her smile and her palate. He's paying as much in as he can possibly afford, as the proceeds arising in six years' time will be enough to set him up in his very own restaurant and keep him going until his customers become regulars.

Jacqueline's unit-linked policy has been going for a long time, ever since she decided to put by some of her catering earnings nine years ago. She's timed her policy to mature when her husband retires at 65. Her premiums may be relatively small but the accumulative effect of her savings over the years should ensure that she and her husband join that gastronomic cruise they've always promised themselves, and that there's still enough left over to keep in a building society* as useful capital.

In addition to laying that nest-egg both Alan and Jacqueline are ensuring that their nearest and dearest will be provided for in the unlikely event of their untimely death. Should Alan have a fatal accident before his policy matures, Pam won't be left penniless; if Jacqueline goes, at least

* See Chapter 14

Patrick will be spared the financial loss that so often follows the bereavement of a wife as well as of a husband.

For every £100 of premium each of them pays in they are getting £17.50 tax relief from the Inland Revenue. Not that they really notice it. For instead of paying the full price of their premiums and claiming the tax relief back afterwards they simply pay the reduced price, or *net premium*, straight to the insurance company. Alan, for example, is now contributing £1000 a year, but only actually paying out £825: his company is automatically crediting him with £175 worth of tax relief.

Patrick meanwhile has gone one better. It was a standing joke that he was hopeless with money and couldn't save even if his life depended on it. Although he took out a life assurance family protection policy when he first set up home, he started to be concerned about his retirement finances only two years ago. His broker advised him to take out both a personal pension plan and a ten-year endowment policy that very day.

Over ten years of saving in these two schemes Patrick can put aside more than three years' earnings, with so much help from the tax-man that he won't be reduced to penury as he saves. Not only will he get 17½ per cent relief on his endowment premiums, he'll get full relief at his highest tax rate on all his personal pension premiums.

Just after he returns from his wife-sponsored cruise he could reap the rewards of both his policies: a tax-free lump sum from his endowment policy, and a tax-free lump sum plus taxable income from his pension scheme.

As a man accustomed to a regular cash inflow, what he really wants is income, not capital. He wants to be able to afford himself: to carry on living—and dining—in much the same way as before. So what he will do is purchase a joint-life annuity with most of the cash that his policies produce.

In fact his eventual income—pension plus annuity—could easily be well over half his original salary: not bad for a mere ten years of painless saving. Some of this will of course go in tax: his pension will be taxable as earned income, and just part of his annuity, the interest part, as unearned income. But all in all the former hopeless saver will have pulled himself up by his bootlaces and gained a fairly prestigious financial reputation within the extremely effervescent Gibson family.

13 'Money is like muck, not good except it be spread'

Bacon: ESSAYS, 15, 'Of Seditions and Troubles'

In 1807 Mr Samuel Whitbread MP, an astute and practical member of the famous brewing family, put before Parliament a most original Bill. He proposed the setting up of a national bank for the labouring classes, to encourage the small-time, short-term saver who valued access to his money as highly as interest on it.

His Bill got precisely nowhere.

Over half a century later, in 1859, an almost identical Bill presented by a Mr William Sikes achieved the success denied to Mr Whitbread. Mr Sikes just happened to be friendly with two of the biggest string-pullers of his day: Sir Rowland Hill, the man who introduced the Penny Post, then Secretary of the Post Office, and William Ewart Gladstone, the GOM himself, then Chancellor of the Exchequer. And so it was that in May 1861 Mr Whitbread's vision became a reality.

The workers flocked to the new bank, and no wonder. Everyone who opened an account, however small, received a yearly interest rate of 2½ per cent, a State guarantee of security, and immediate access to his money whenever he wanted it back.

The bank was then known as the Post Office Savings Bank. Nowadays we call it the National Savings Bank as it forms part of the Department for National Savings. It pays rather better interest rates now than it once did, but it's still an ultra-secure and most accessible place to keep moderate sums of money. As such it's a prime example of a completely different type of granary needed by the self-employed. When they're doing their best to ensure that their major, long-term savings are as cost-effective as possible, it would be ludicrous for them to ignore the potential of their non-committed money—readily available though it may have to be—by leaving it to moulder in jam-jars and current accounts.

You can open an *ordinary* National Savings Bank account with as little as 25p at any one of over 20,000 Post Offices throughout the country, pay in and withdraw your money more or less at will, and receive interest at 5 per cent per annum on every pound you save for a full calendar month. What's more, the first £70 worth of interest will be free of all income tax, so you can have up to £1400 in your account with no tax to pay whatsoever.

The Government alone can offer valuable tax concessions such as this. They crop up in some of the other short-term investment schemes run by the Department for National Savings, available from banks as well as post offices.

National Savings Certificates are the prime example. The current 18th issue, though based upon a five-year minimum savings period, could actually be used to produce a tax-free yield at any time after an initial twelve months is up. The longer you can afford to leave your certificates untouched, however, the higher your tax-free interest rate will be: 5 per cent per annum during the first year, 7.14 per cent over the second, 8.8 per cent during the third year, 10.29 per cent during the fourth year and 11.11 per cent for the fifth. Since the minimum purchase is a mere £10, almost any tax-payer could afford to exploit this concession, however small his holding.

Save As You Earn, or SAYE, is another scheme with tax advantages, this time based upon a five- or seven-year savings period, but once again capable of providing a tax-free return after only twelve months. The idea of the current index-linked third issue is that you save a sum of money, between £4 and £20, regularly every month for five years. Each contribution will be linked to the Retail Prices Index to preserve its purchasing power, so that after five years are up your tax-free investment return will be equal to average price rises over those years. Leave your money untouched for a further two years, and you'll get a tax-free bonus, equal to two monthly contributions, as well as a further revaluation. Cease your payments after a year and you'll get a tax-free interest rate of six per cent per annum instead of the index-linking.

Then of course *Premium Savings Bonds*, though perhaps a rather chancy investment medium, are graced with a major tax concession. Should you be lucky enough to hit the £100,000 jackpot — or any of the lesser sums — with one of your bonds, your prize will be free of all income and capital gains tax. Although an investment consultant would probably frown on a scheme whose return depended entirely on the whims of an electronic winner-picker known as Ernie, Premium Bonds are in fact a more advisable home for your

ERNIE
KZH/937 046
PAY
100.000-//

spare cash than fruit machines, vingt-et-un, bingo and the pools. For even if you don't win, at least you don't lose: every £5 worth of bonds that you buy can always be cashed without penalty.

With all these flexible, short-term, profitably tax-free granaries available you should have no excuse for letting your liquid assets stagnate. You could try a small holding in each, experiment a little, spread your money around as Bacon advised. Or you might keep an eye open for other, comparable schemes which may just be more convenient or advantageous for you.

During the early years of the nineteenth century, as Mr Whitbread was preparing his resounding failure, a canny Scots minister, Dr Henry Duncan, was preaching economy and thrift to his flock in a desolate backwood of Dumfriesshire.

His canniness was surpassed only by the uncanny effect of his oratorical display, for from his dramatic exhortations sprang the first in a long line of *Trustee Savings Banks.*

Right from the first, Trustee Savings Banks have been separate, non-profit-making units administered by unpaid local trustees and managers. Nowadays, however, each bank comes under government supervision, and the fixed interest rates, together with the deposits on which they are paid, are guaranteed by the State.

It is hardly surprising, therefore, that a Trustee Savings Bank *ordinary department account* bears a family resemblance to a National Savings Bank ordinary account.

Interest on deposits is a fixed four per cent per annum, with the first £70 worth free of all tax. Subsequent deposits and reasonable cash withdrawals are again no problem—arrangements can be made with any other Trustee Savings Bank.

Although Trustee Savings Banks pay one per cent less interest than the National Savings Bank, they provide a much greater range of services than the Department for National Savings as a whole. In fact they combine many of the facilities of both the National Savings Department and a 'normal' High Street bank.

Almost all of them provide cheque accounts and carry out the routine transactions you'd associate with major banks. All of them participate in the SAYE scheme as well as the National Giro system. And every one of them possesses Special Investment and Government Stock departments where all interest payable on deposits is liable to tax—as is the case with some National Savings schemes.

Since all these services are so conveniently grouped together under one roof as in some huge investment supermarket, you may easily find it more agreeable to spread your particular muck around the supermarket's different departments . . . .

14 'Save a boy friend for a rainy day-and another, in case it doesn't rain'

(Mae West)

Two centuries ago there was a chronic housing shortage at Golden Cross, Birmingham. Too many citizens were living cheek by jowl with their in-laws and right under the noses of their neighbours. The situation was ripe for revolution.

The revolutionaries turned out to be a peaceful group of artisans and higher-paid manual workers. Although they took the law into their own hands it was merely in order to found a radical and innovative housing club.

Each member of this club undertook to pay a regular fixed 'share' into its coffers. When these were brimming over, the accumulated funds were used to buy up building land and subsequently to erect individual houses on it. As each house neared completion the members drew lots for it; the lucky strawholder could then either kiss his mother-in-law goodbye and move in, or, should her home cooking prove indispensable to his well-being, sell his rights or shares to another member. All members, winners or losers, continued to fork out their contributions until everyone had a house.

This club was known as Ketley's Building Society.

Building Societies nowadays, though obviously more sophisticated than they were in 1775, are still based on the original Ketley concept: the savings of investing members are used to help borrowing members buy or build their own homes. And just as before, an investing member doesn't need to end up with a house himself if he doesn't want one. The sophistication lies in the variety of schemes now offered to the investor, often confusingly given different names by different societies.

Most societies offer one or more versions of three main types of savings plan. The first is the 'any amount-any time-easy withdrawals' type; the second requires regular monthly contributions; the third is of the 'lump sum-fixed term' kind. What they all have in common is that the interest that accrues is paid free of basic rate income tax, currently 33 per cent. If you happen to be a higher rate tax-payer you'll have to pay extra tax. And if you don't pay tax at all you can't claim back the tax paid by the society on your behalf. Building Society accounts are therefore not ideal granaries for any investor not paying basic rate tax.

A modern self-employed artisan, paying basic rate tax and still searching for that short-term, flexible savings plan, need look no further than the first type of scheme on offer: the *ordinary* or *paid-up share account*.

An ordinary share account can be opened with as little as £1 but may hold as much as £15,000 at any one time. Money may be paid in and taken out more or less at will, though a few days' notice would be needed for large withdrawals. The usual net interest rate on share accounts is currently 8 per cent — the figure set by the Building Societies Association* to which the majority of societies belong. This net figure, and the ones given below, shows the return to a basic rate income tax payer. Those who pay higher rate tax or the investment income surcharge will receive a lower net return.

Should our artisan, however, have a steady income which would allow for a regular monthly saving of anything up to £50 — so long as funds remained easily accessible — he

* See the address list at the back of the book.

might care to try a scheme from the second type on offer. A *savings plan* or *subscription share account* will pay a higher net interest rate, currently 9.25 per cent, but will still, in some instances, enable him to get at his savings whenever he needs to.

It is only when he can commit his money for a minimum period of time that he can participate in the other sort of scheme available within the second group. Here even higher interest rates are paid because the regular monthly contributions are left untouched for three, five or seven years. SAYE schemes crop up here, yielding a net 8.62 per cent over a seven-year period.

For the time being he need not even consider the *investment certificate* and *term share accounts* of the third group: these require a capital outlay of at least £500 or £1000 which must remain untouched for a two- or three-year period to produce a net interest rate of 8.5 per cent or 9 per cent per annum.

As you can see, as short-term granaries for the basic-rate tax-payer the first two types of Building Society account are more profitable than ordinary department accounts in both National Savings and Trustee Savings Banks. What's more, they offer an investor the very valuable possibility of his society granting him a mortgage on his house. Even if he has no immediate intention of buying a property, his account stands as his provision for that rainy day some time in the future when a home loan might be just what he needs.

Should this rainy day never arrive, however, the investor may well realise in retrospect that he could have done better still with yet another short-term savings scheme, to be found on the other side of the lending fence: the *Local Authority loan.*

Local authorities up and down the country are almost constantly on the look-out for capital as well as for old newspapers and washed milk bottle tops. They need the money to finance buildings, re-cycling plants and services and amenities of all kinds within their geographical confines. Their need is often urgent.

There are always some local authorities around who choose to raise capital by offering very attractive interest rates to anyone willing to lend them a minimum of £200 or £500 for a certain minimum period of time: this could be two years, or five or six. Unfortunately their rates are *gross* and the interest is taxable, but the current *net* yield for a basic rate tax-payer is still not to be sneezed at: a minimum 7 per cent for a two-year loan and a minimum 8 per cent for a five-year loan. Should his fortunes change for the worse and his tax rate plummet to zero, he will of course reap the full benefits of double figure rates.

Local authorities normally advertise their particular deals fairly extensively in local papers and civic centres; some go as far as the national press. However for a fully comprehensive and up to date list of all borrowing boroughs you need to apply to the Chartered Institute of Public Finance and Accountancy.*

The list of short-term granaries does not actually peter out here, but the alternatives often involve an element of risk, and require the kind of financial commitment and

* See the address list at the back of the book.

combination of qualities and virtues with which the average self-employed person wouldn't even wish to be associated. Bernard M. Baruch summed up the situation in his advice on how to grow wealthy through stock speculation:

'If you are ready and able to give up everything else, and will study the market and every stock listed there as carefully as a medical student studies anatomy, and will glue your nose to the ticker tape at the opening of every day of the year and never take it off till night; if you can do all that, and in addition have the cool nerve of a gambler, the sixth sense of a clairvoyant and the courage of a lion—you have a Chinaman's chance'.

Glossary

For further information on an entry, try the page(s) mentioned.

ACTUARY: An expert in mathematics and the theory of risk who calculates pension and life assurance premiums and bonuses.

ADDITIONAL LIFE ASSURANCE: Term life assurance protection for the family of a personal pension policy-holder against his premature death. This can be either an optional extra incorporated into his pension policy, or a completely separate financial arrangement. Subject to Inland Revenue limits he should get tax relief on all his relevant premiums at the highest rate of tax he pays. See pages 66-8.

ANNUITY: An income, usually payable for life, bought either with a single premium lump sum, or a series of premiums. In the case of a single premium payment it can be *immediate*— starting straight away after your payment. Otherwise it is *deferred*— starting after a certain period of time has elapsed. In most cases it is treated as a 'purchased life annuity', and only part of your income is taxable (the interest, not the capital repayment). Annuities can also be arranged for a couple so that the income continues for the rest of both of their lives. Deferred annuities are the basis of all pension schemes. See pages 25-35.

BASIC RETIREMENT PENSION: The first-tier State pension, applicable to all classes of National Insurance contributor, including the self-employed. It is currently paying out a maximum £19.50 a week at retirement to a single person. See page 20.

CAPITAL TRANSFER TAX: A tax imposed when capital totalling over £25,000 changes hands by way of gift or at death. If any death benefit from your personal pension policy brings your total estate up above this figure, your heir or beneficiary will in theory have to pay capital transfer tax on it. However, by leaving the death benefit to your spouse, or as an annuity to another beneficiary, you could avoid any such liability. See pages 63-7.

COMMUTATION: The valuable right to exchange part of your personal pension for a tax-free cash sum. This must not exceed three times the remaining pension. See page 56.

CONTROLLING DIRECTOR: A person who owns or controls more than 5 per cent of the voting equity of a director-controlled company. He can take out a self-employed retirement annuity or, under the Finance Act of 1973, he can join his own company's pension scheme.

DEPOSIT ADMINISTRATION SCHEME: To the investor this is the same as a with-profits pension scheme although the profits will be worked out in a slightly different way. See pages 39, 43.

DISABILITY: In addition to buying, if he wishes, an individual permanent health insurance policy from a life office, a personal pension policy-holder can sometimes guard against losing his pension through incapacity by paying a small extra premium. See pages 72-3.

DYNAMIC PENSION: One that starts at a lower level than a fixed pension but gives you value for money by continuing to share in company profits throughout your retirement. The name is sometimes used to describe an escalating pension. See over.

ENDOWMENT POLICY: An investment type of life assurance policy under which a minimum pre-arranged sum of money—often together with investment profits of some sort—is payable when the scheme ends or at the prior death of the policy-holder. An endowment policy can often reinforce a personal pension scheme, although its limited tax concessions prevent it from being a suitable substitute. See pages 68,76-80.

ESCALATING PENSION: One that starts at a lower level than a fixed pension but increases steadily by a certain percentage rate throughout your retirement. See page 57.

FINAL BONUS: See TERMINAL BONUS.

FINAL PAY SCHEME: An occupational pension scheme in which an employee's pension is related to his salary just prior to retirement. See page 72.

INLAND REVENUE LIMITS: The highest premium levels permitted by the Inland Revenue for full tax concessions. See pages 58-62, 75,78.

INVESTMENT INCOME SURCHARGE: An additional tax imposed on investment income exceeding £1700 (or £2500 in the case of beneficiaries aged 65 and over). See pages 59, 93.

JOINT-LIFE AND SURVIVOR PENSION: A pension payable to the policy-holder and his spouse for the rest of both of their lives. See pages 68-9, 82.

LIFE OFFICE: Another name for a life assurance company. See page 40.

MEDICAL: A personal pension policy-holder wishing to protect his dependants by taking out a term life assurance policy may need to provide his company (at their expense) with medical evidence of his good health. See page 67.

MINIMUM GUARANTEED PENSION: The basic or underlying pension is guaranteed to be not less than a specified annual amount. See pages 42, 48.

MINIMUM GUARANTEED PERIOD: The specified number of years, usually five but occasionally ten, during which your pension will be paid out, whether you're there to receive it or not. This guarantee may be a feature of your scheme or an optional extra. See pages 57, 64.

NATIONAL INSURANCE BENEFITS: The fund into which you make your National Insurance payments will eventually provide you with a variety of State benefits, provided that the normal contribution conditions are fulfilled. Self-employed contributions count towards the following benefits: flat-rate *sickness benefit, invalidity benefit, maternity benefit,* basic *widow's benefit,* basic *retirement pension, child's special allowance* and *death grant*. Under no circumstances can you be eligible for unemployment or industrial injuries benefits, or earnings-related sickness, widow's or retirement benefit. If your income is inadequate to support you, you may also apply for *supplementary benefit* (if you are not working full-time) or *family income supplement* (if you are working full-time and have at least one child in your family). Explanatory leaflets on all these benefits are obtainable from your local social security office. See pages 20-2.

NON-PROFIT SCHEME: One which pays a prearranged annual amount of pension at retirement. See pages 39, 41.

OCCUPATIONAL PENSION: Another way of saying firms' or companies' pensions. See pages 40,72.

PAID-UP PENSION: The pension your premiums have secured up to the time you abandon your personal pension policy. This pension remains 'frozen' until it is paid out to you at retirement, usually together with additional bonuses or investment profits of some kind. See pages 53,71-2.

PAY-AS-YOU-GO: A funding system, such as that of the State pension scheme, whereby your contributions secure not your own future benefits but benefits currently being paid out. Your State pension (if you're not yet retired) will come from payments made by future generations of contributors.

PERMANENT HEALTH INSURANCE SCHEME: A policy bought from a life office which protects the policy-holder against sickness or disability. A pre-agreed number of weeks after he falls ill he starts to receive a regular income which continues until he is fit to recommence work or until the policy expires, whichever is the sooner. Women pay higher premiums than men for the same amount of income.

PERSONAL PENSION PLAN: A private pension arrangement between an individual who is not a member of an occupational pension scheme and a life office. Those with two sources of income, one of which does not carry pension rights, may also be eligible. See page 39, *et seq*.

PREMIUMS: The contribution(s) required to provide your annuity, or your pension and other benefits, calculated by an actuary bearing in mind such details as your age and sex, as well as investment returns, mortality rates etc. There are several types of premium: monthly, annual, single, varying and so on. See pages 46-7, 52-3.

REFUND OF PREMIUMS: If a personal pension policy-holder dies before retirement his gross premiums are usually returned to his estate or dependants, often with a certain amount of compound interest or investment profits of some kind. Should the sum be substantial, it may be payable in the form of a pension to his widow or other nominee. See page 66.

RETIREMENT AGE: Retirement age within the State pension scheme is a minimum of 65 for men and 60 for women, with up to five years' postponement being allowed. Personal pension retirement age can be anywhere between 60 and 75, or even earlier in special cases. See pages 23, 54-5.

REVERSIONARY BONUS: Only applicable to a with-profits pension scheme. Each policy-holder shares in his company's profits by getting periodic reversionary bonuses tacked on to his minimum guaranteed pension (or minimum cash equivalent). These bonuses are added on every one to three years, whenever the company works out its surplus—and each individual's share of this surplus. They may be 'simple' or 'compound'; 'simple' meaning that they are based only on the minimum guaranteed sum, 'compound' meaning that they are based on this sum plus any bonuses already added. See pages 42-3.

SELF-EMPLOYED RETIREMENT ANNUITY: See PERSONAL PENSION PLAN.

SICKNESS: See DISABILITY and PERMANENT HEALTH INSURANCE SCHEME.

SINGLE PREMIUMS: Personal pension policies may be bought on a year-by-year basis with a series of single premiums. These attract tax relief in the same way as regular premiums and allow for considerable flexibility of payment. Immediate annuities are also purchased with a single lump sum premium. See pages 52-3.

STATE PENSIONABLE AGE: See RETIREMENT AGE.

TAX: Retirement pensions are taxable as earned income. Immediate annuities however are only partly taxable, but the relevant interest part is treated as unearned or investment income and potentially taxable at a higher rate. See pages 58-9.

TAX RELIEF: Tax relief at the highest rate paid by the policy-holder is allowed on all premiums in personal pension schemes, provided Inland Revenue limits are not exceeded. An endowment assurance policy-holder can get 17½ per cent tax relief on that portion of his yearly premium which constitutes less than one-sixth of his annual income or a monetary ceiling of £1500, whichever is the greater. Other savings schemes offering valuable tax concessions are to be found within the Department for National Savings and Trustee Savings Banks. See pages 58-63, 81.

TERMINAL BONUS: A final bonus is occasionally added at the end of a with-profits pension scheme, reflecting any company surplus not yet credited to you in the form of reversionary bonuses. See page 43.

TERM ASSURANCE: A low-cost protection-only life assurance policy. An agreed sum of money, the 'sum assured', is usually paid out to your family if you die within a specified period, the 'term' of the policy. Occasionally you may insure someone else's life over a period of years, provided you have a valid financial interest in his continuing survival. See pages 66-8.

UNIT-LINKED PENSION: A scheme in which most of your pension premium money is linked directly to various units in an investment fund, your pension being almost entirely dependent on how well these investments perform. Usually your income at retirement is based on the value of your units at that time, but you may have the option of keeping your pension unit-linked even after it starts to pay out. See pages 45-9.

UNTIED CASH OPTION: A new rule which allows each personal pension policy-holder to transfer the cash equivalent of the retirement annuity his company offers him to another company which offers a higher rate of annuity (provided the first company agrees). See page 56.

VESTING BONUS: See TERMINAL BONUS.

WIDOWS: See ADDITIONAL LIFE ASSURANCE and JOINT-LIFE AND SURVIVOR PENSION.

WILLS: It is difficult to overstress the importance of making a will to avoid delay, disappointment and financial distress at your decease. It is advisable to have your will drawn up by a solicitor who, through his expertise, may more than repay his legal costs.

WITH-PROFITS SCHEME: One which entitles the policy-holder to a share in his company's profits. This comes in the form of periodic bonuses added on to his minimum guaranteed pension (or cash equivalent). See pages 39, 42-4.

Address List

The Department of Health and Social Security, Headquarters Offices,
Alexander Fleming House,
Elephant and Castle,
London SE1 6BY
(01-407 5522)

The National Federation of the Self-Employed,
St Anne's Road West,
Lytham St Annes,
Lancashire

The Association of Self-Employed People,
279 Church Road,
London SE19 2QQ
(01-653 4798)

The Pre-Retirement Association,
19 Undine Street,
Tooting,
London SW17 8PP

British Insurance Brokers' Association,
Fountain House,
130 Fenchurch Street,
London EC3M 5DJ,
(01-623 9043)

Lloyd's Insurance Brokers' Association,
Lloyd's Building,
Lime Street,
London EC3M 7HA
(01-623 2855)

Life Offices' Association (and Industrial Life Offices' Association),
Aldermanbury House,
Queen Street,
London EC4N 1TP
(01-236 5117, 01-248 4477)

Associated Scottish Life Offices,
23 St Andrew Square,
Edinburgh EH2 1AQ
(031-556 7171)

The Director of Savings,
The National Savings Bank,
Glasgow GS8 1SB

The Building Societies Association,
14 Park Street,
London W1
(01-629 0515)

The Chartered Institute of Public Finance and Accountancy,
232 Vauxhall Bridge Road,
London SW1
(01-828 7855)

More detailed information on comparative personal pension schemes and other savings plans may be obtained through the following publications:

The Savings Market (a quarterly subscription magazine)
Money Management and Unitholder (a monthly subscription magazine)
The Economist
The Investors Chronicle and Stock Exchange Gazette
and the financial pages of many national newspapers.